WE FOUR, AND THE STORIES WE TOLD.

BY
HENRY LAPHAM,

Edited by Marolyn Diver

Many thanks to the following people for their help, guidance and expertise.

David Dudfield, Francie & Peter Diver.

Notes:

The original spelling and phrasing has been kept to preserve the character of the author's narratives.

Dornie Publishing Company

Grasmere, Invercargill

www.dorniepublishing.tk

Original text 1880 © Henry Lapham

2012 Edition © Marolyn Diver

Images © named individuals, institutions.
All rights reserved

ISBN 978-0-473-21946-8

Cover design by Strawberrymouse Designs

Published under the Creative Commons Attribution-Share Alike 3.0 New Zealand Licence

Introduction

Henry Lapham

Henry Lapham

Henry Lapham was born in Tasmania in 1852.. He followed his big sister and fellow writer Susan Nugent Wood to the goldfields of Victoria, Australia then onwards to Waikaia, New Zealand. There he spent some time seeking his fortune over nearly every active "rush" in Otago and Southland until he settled down to be a school teacher in the Waikaia township. Over this time he wrote many short stories based on his adventures and made a large contribution to the *Otago Witness*, writing a regular column that was very successful. He and his sister eventually combined their talent and published *Waiting for the Mail - and other sketches and poems* in 1875. Henry went on to produce his own work with this publication of *We Four and the Stories We Told* inspired by one night he and his fellow "diggers" told thrilling stories by a fireside.

For a while he took on a private teaching job with a wealthy family and moved up to the North Island only to find that his health declined. It was discovered that Henry suffered from tuberculosis. He eventually returned to teaching in Waikaia but his health never returned and he died after a six month struggle at Invercargill hospital in 1887 aged 35. He never married or had children and he is buried in a small family plot at St. Johns Cemetery, Invercargill alongside his sister and her husband.

Gold on the Waikaia

The main Switzers gold rush, around which many of these stories are set, began in November 1861 near present day Waikaia. Miners had located the precious metal through diligent prospecting around the margins of the Tuapeka (Lawrence) and Dunstan (Alexandra) goldfields in Central Otago. Neighbouring goldfields were also discovered further north along the Waikaia valley at Campbells and Potters.

Perhaps due to the richer fields in Otago, news of this discovery was not widely publicised until later in 1862. Nevertheless one of the first public reports of the Waikaia goldfield provided directions to the site, information about the nature of the gold and suggested good returns could be had[1].

By the end of the 1862 there were 400 miners working at Campbells and Potters with 200 more at Switzers; a few months later in April 1863 there were 700 miners reported at Switzers alone.

These miners required food and equipment on the goldfields, as well as entertainment and lodgings when in town. Fairly soon the township of Switzers became established on the low hills east of present day Waikaia. Within a few years the township boasted a population of 2000, a cobbled main street, courthouse, church, school, assorted tradesmen, retailers and merchants. However Switzers was also a typical rough and ready mining town with gambling dens, dancing halls and a high ratio of drinking establishments per head of population[2].

Unfortunately for the township the alluvial gold didn't last and within a couple of decades the prosperity of Switzers had began to noticeably decline. A new township, Waikaia, was surveyed

---

[1] Otago Daily Times, 14 October 1862. "The prospectors' claim has proved to yield about half a pennyweight to the pan of coarse gold, with 2 feet of wash dirt, and a soft slaty bottom."

[2] Miller (1966:21) suggested every third or fourth house in Switzers was a "pub or shanty" at the height of the gold rush.

on the flat ground (but still above flood levels) to the west of Switzers and much of the old township was sluiced away. Many European miners decided to prospect elsewhere and sold their claims to Chinese miners.

By the mid 1880s there were only 374 miners at Switzers, comprised of 254 Chinese and 121 Europeans. In the late 19th – early 20th century dredging became the main method of gold extraction in the valley; the last major productive claim was King Solomon's Mine to the east of Waikaia and it was closed in 1937.

Map of Waikaia and part of Wart Hill Survey Districts, 1889.

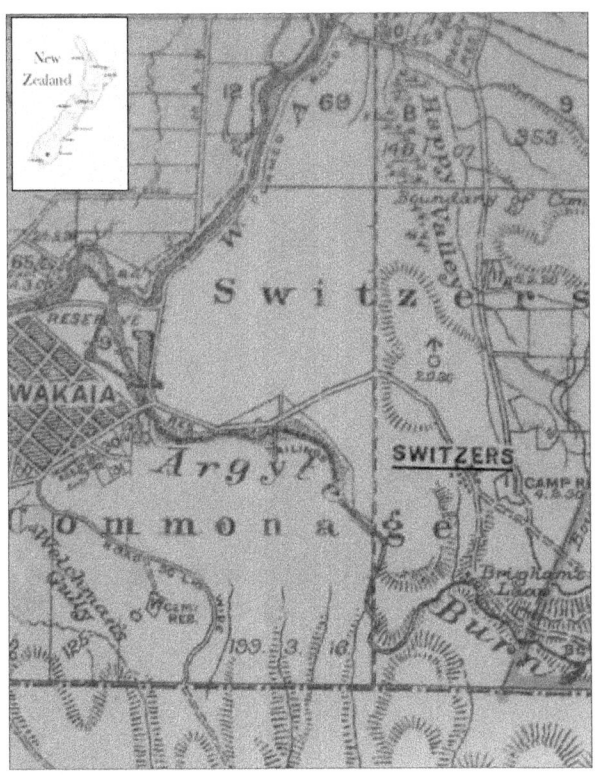

Contents

1. FRIGHTENED BY A BABY....................11
Jack Conliffe's Story.

2. QUEER!...16
Harry Clare's Story.

3. A MEMBER OF THE FORCE.............25
Archie Black's Story.

4. THE PATER'S GHOST STORY........45
My Own Contribution.

BY WAY OF PROLOGUE.

by
Henry Lapham

WE FOUR were Jack Conliffe, Harry Clare, Archie Black, and I. We were seated in a hotel parlour on a winter night. We had played cards till we were tired, and now sat talking fitfully.

At last I said, "It will be very dark for you, boys, going home tonight. Take care you don't come to grief crossing over the Creek, or see a ghost; it is just the night for such things to be abroad."

"I recollect going home one pitch dark night," said Archie, "after listening to a lot of ghost and murder stories, and suddenly I tumbled over a white calf. The brute got up in a hurry with a most unearthly bellow, and I really thought my hair was 'turned all white.' I don't believe I was ever so startled before."

This led the conversation to the subjects of frights in general......

FRIGHTENED BY A BABY

———————◆———————

"FRIGHTS!" said Jack Conliffe, blowing a long whiff from his pipe,"well, I've had some queer frights in my time, but the greatest I ever got was from a baby!"

"And no wonder," said Harry Clare, "it's enough to scare any one, particularly when they come unexpected." Harry, by the bye, was a married man and lately the father of twins.

"As to that," retorted Jack, "you can speak from experience and ought to know, but it wasn't in that way I got my scare."

"Tell us all about it, Jack!" said the rest of us, as we replenished our pipes and drew round the cheerful fire in the parlour.

"Well," said Jack, "you know when the first Commissioner came to *The Creek* his eldest boy was only a kid, about two years old maybe, but he was as sensible as a daddy of fifty. First time I saw him was one morning as I was going to work, and took the track round by the Camp. Not much of a place neither was the Camp in those days, not a bit better than many a place in the township. It was a canvass tent, 10 by 12, and they did their cooking outside. The bobby had another little tent further on, and the ground was enclosed with a sod fence. Well, as I was a saying, I went round by the camp, and at the gate I saw the missus a-watching for the Commissioner, who had gone up the Creek to look for the horse.

'Good morning, ma'am,' says I.

'Good morning,' says she, with a smile that was as good as a blink of sunshine on a cloudy day—she was a real lady, you bet. 'Have you seen anything of my husband?' she asked.

'Yes,' says I, 'he's just a-driving the horse home. And how's the young commissioner?'

'Oh, thank you, he's very well.'

'Will you come to me, my lad?' says I to the boy, who she had in her arms. And I'm blest to goodness! If he didn't hold out his hands as ready as could be.

Well, I took him of course. At first he held back, as if to make sure what kind of creature had got hold of him, then he gets friendly and fixes his hands in my beard. And you bet, boys, but he could pull. It was all meant for fun I daresay, but it was sore, very sore. I felt my face getting red, and for the life of me I could not keep the tears out of my eyes. You see," added Jack, in an apologetic tone, "I ain't accustomed to youngsters."

"Well, his mother wanted to take him away, but not a bit would he go. So I said I would take him for a walk. I put him on my back, and he grabbed hold of the collar of my shirt, sticking his heels into my ribs and singing out, 'Gee, gee,' and him not two years old! Well, I took him down the flat, and a good three miles afore we reached the camp again, and him a-chirping and a-kicking as merry as a cricket all the time. When we got home there was the boss, and as soon as the youngster saw his dad he was off. After that I got into a sort of habit of going to see the boy every two or three days. He was such a real jolly little chap.

So it went on till Christmas came. Now the youngster's birthday was either just before or just after Christmas, we were not sure which, but we before or just after Christmas, we were not sure which, but we made up our minds that some of us would club together and give the young'un a good Christmas Box. Why, half the fellows on the creek knew and was fond of that boy. Well, we got a box, ornamental you know, and in it we put a lot of pretty fair specimens. Now we thought it wouldn't do for a lot of us to go crowding up to the camp, so we formed a committee, and they were to take the box on X'mas morning and give it to the kid. I was one of the committee, and as I knew the boy first and best I was to make the present.

Well, when we got to the camp that morning who should come toddling to the door but the very youngster himself. He looked at us sort of frightened like at first, but when he sees me he called out, 'Yak,' as plain as could be, and him never spoke a blessed word afore! His mother came out presently and wished us 'Merry Christmas,' but she couldn't believe it about baby.

"Just you try him, ma'am," says I; so she brought him up to me, and asks him,

'Who is this, baby?'

'Yak,' says he, as if he knew all about it. Well, to be sure, the missus was as pleased as pleased, and then the Commissioner came out and the boy had to do it over again. The boss did not say much, but bless you, he looked as proud as Punch. Then we told them about the box, and if it had been £20,000 worth they could not have been more pleased. Then the Commissioner brought out brandy and whisky, and we drank 'Health and long life to the Young 'Un,' and each of their healths and I believe each of our own, too; at any rate we were pretty well on afore we left the camp, and after that I never saw daylight for four days. Not that it mattered much, for it rained very nearly all the time, and the snow melted on the ranges and the creek rose very high. Well, towards the end of the week I cleared out for home. In those days the only bridge across the creek was just a plank laid over and chained to keep it fast at both ends, and it sloped down at a pretty sharp incline from one side to the other. It needed a good steady head to walk that plank, I tell you. Well, the water had been running over it for days during the last flood, and I didn't half like the idea of crossing on it, though the flood had gone down. But when I got over the flat and beside the creek I'm blessed to goodness! But I thought the sight would leave my eyes, for there at the further end of the plank what should I see but the young Commissioner. Yes, there he was, squatting on all fours, a-laughing and a-chirping at the water that surged and foamed with a current swift enough to sweep away a grown man, let alone a child. I've been in many a queer fix, boys, but never another like this. I darn't sing out for fear of startling him, and I couldn't, nor could any man, cross that stream on foot. I can't swim a stroke if it was to save my life.

There I stood like a fool and did not know what to be at. And there was the kid, his curly golden head bent down and his pretty baby face a-smiling at the water. Well, after a bit, he crawls on slowly and steadily into the middle of the plank.

There he stopped, and, I suppose, got frightened at something, the slope down of the plank, may be; any way, he began to cry, but, good Lord, mates, I thought it was all over when I saw him trying to turn round. I must do something I knew, so I commenced to whistle softly. He put his head on one side to listen, then looked up, and laughing through his tears, sang out, quite jolly, 'Yak?'

'That's right, my boy,' says I, 'come along to Jack, steady now,' and I goes to the end of the plank, holding out my arms. But what do you think he did? I'm blessed to goodness if he didn't stand up! Yes, right straight up on those tottering baby legs of his, and tried to walk. To walk along that there sloping plank over a boiling, rushing, stream— him as could scarcely walk along a level floor without a fall! Well, he came on pretty steady for a good bit, and me holding out my hands and shaking like a blessed old woman. Well, he got on first-rate until he was three or four yards from the end of the plank, then if he didn't break into a trot. I felt as weak and sick as a fainting girl as he came on, getting faster and faster with the slope of the plank; but he was right until pretty near the end, when his foot slipped, and he fell—but it was into my arms, mates, else I wouldn't be here telling the story.

Well, when I had him right I set to a-hugging him and a-dancing round like a blamed old idiot. Then I tried to carry him home. But it wouldn't do. Two steps on the plank turned me dizzy. So I went back to the United States Hotel, and as soon as I came into the bar, the missus said,-

"Why, Jack, you look as white as chalk! What's the matter? Have you been seeing a ghost?'

'No, says I, but I've been seeing a baby, and that's a blamed sight worse; give me a big 'nip,' old woman.' And for all her asking I wouldn't tell her any more. I didn't want the boy's mother to know about it; and I knew if I told the woman it would soon be over all the township. Women can't keep a secret, and the more you tell them to keep it quiet the sooner they'll go and whisper it. It's their nature, poor things, so you can't blame 'em. Well, when I did get the boy home, there was his mother in an awful way, for she had missed him.

'Oh, where did you find him?' says she.

'I found him playing down by the creek,' says I, 'and a real dangerous place it is, ma'am, just now."

'Oh dear, dear! What an escape! Why, he might have tumbled in,' says she; 'Oh, you naughty, naughty, boy.'

"And then she began a-kissing him very hard for punishment, I suppose. "Well, thought I to myself, I wouldn't mind having a nice young woman a-punishing me all day long,' but I only said, 'Well, good morning, now, ma'am.'

'Good morning, Jack,' says she, putting her slim, white, dainty hand into my big paw, 'and many thanks for your kindness in bringing home this bad boy.'

"But she never heard the rights of the story to this day."

QUEER!

"TALKING about Babies," said Harry Clare, the father of twins, "I mind a strange adventure we had with one of ours."

"Which of 'em was it?" asked Jack Conliffe.

"Well, let me see," said Harry, reflectively, "I think it was Johnny: no, but it couldn't, for now I mind it was a girl. Then, perhaps it was Mary Ann, or, let me see, it might have been Sally, or maybe, Dick,—oh! but that's a boy again, well, I think it was Sally. You see, mates, when a man has a dozen or more of 'em it isn't always easy to say which is which, but the missis, she knows."

"They are a pretty regular annual event, ain't they?" queries young Archie Black, as he stretched his brawny limbs towards the fire.

"Yes," admitted Harry, mournfully, "pretty regular, and this time, good Heavens, it's twins!" His dismay and terror at this unlooked-for catastrophe was so evident that Archie Black, with a consideration that did honour to his bachelorhood, immediately called for "drinks." A glass restored Harry's equanimity, and enabled him to continue his story.

"Well, when first we came to the Creek there wasn't a house or tent to be had for love or money, so I spoke to the boys and asked them to lend a hand to put up a sod hut, for it was about the time for an 'annual event,' and the missis didn't care about staying in the rowdy shanty. I shan't forget how those boys stuck to me and worked like niggers, but some of them were married men, and could understand. Well, we got the roof on, but very little more, when the missis was moved in and the baby was born. A real pretty wee girl she was, and I was proud of her too.

"You see, mates," he added apologetically, "this was only our second or third. I don't feel quite so much pride about it now."

The men nodded to show they understood he had grown wiser; then Harry went on.

"May be some of you mind that idiot boy of Barton's? No? Well, it is ten or twelve years since, but there are people on the Creek still who could tell you about him. I don't know why parents keep those deformed poor creatures. It's not right. It's against nature. If a calf comes to light with two heads or five legs don't people always put them out of the way? Unless they keep 'em for a show and turn an honest penny with them. But Barton never could show his. Why, the thing was so infernally ugly, I don't think you'd get any one to look at it if you paid them. What was it like? Well, though only about ten years old it was as big and strong as a boy of fourteen, it had no forehead to speak of, a flat nose, a wide ugly mouth, and small sharp eyes. His head was covered with coarse red hair that grew down almost to his eyelashes, and his head was sunk down between the shoulders.

It had only one arm, the other was nothing but a stump, but with this arm it could climb and tear, and do the deuce's own mischief, and it couldn't speak, no, not a blessed syllable, only yabber and scream. The first time I ever saw the boy was one evening I went to Barton's —the missis and he were out—so as I had a parcel for them and the door was ajar I thought I would leave it on the table. There was a good fire on, and lying in front of it was what I took to be a dog. I went over and gave it a push with my foot. Now, boys, I ain't generally nervous, so to speak, but when this thing sprang up with a yell, its eyes glaring, its red hair on end, its ugly mouth yabbering and gaping, and the stump of an arm going up and down, I did think I'd trodden on the devil. I jumped back, and he came limping up to me, for he had a club foot, and clawed at the buttons on my coat. They were made of brass, and shining. I let him finger them, but when he went for a knife to cut them off, I cleared. Yes, if I'd been Barton I'd have drowned that boy as soon as he was born."

"'Well,' said Archie, '"you see you could spare half a dozen, and perhaps he had only the one.'

"Yes, there's something in that, Archie, there's something in in that, and I doubt if I could spare any of mine, for all that there's thirteen of 'em now with the twins. Well, as I was saying, that was the first time I saw Barton's idiot, though I had heard of it often enough. Well, when the missis was laid up, Mrs. Barton offered to come and look after the children.

"That's real kind of you," says I, "and my missis will be main pleased; but, no offence, Mrs. Barton, only don't bring him with you.

'You mean Peter,' says she, speaking a little short and sharp.

"And it's true, boys, they had actually gone and given a christened name to a thing like that. Isn't it terrible what some fond folks will do?

"Oh, very well,' says she, 'I'll take care he don't get in.'

"And come she did every day, though it was a goodish step where she lived to our place across the creek, and I had spoken rough about Peter—but Mrs. Barton was a real kind creature, she was. Now it was a strange thing about the boy, but he was very fond of children—the younger the better. He would never harm or bite them as he would do to grown folk when he was put out, but play with them as nice as possible, and after a bit the children would take to him too, just as I've seen some youngsters in the gardens at home go and play with the big monkeys; but I never could abide them. As I was saying, Mrs. Barton came every day, and the boy was left outside. He used to carry the youngsters about, and hop along with the club foot, and be as lively as you please.

"One day it was awfully warm, and when Mrs. Barton was going home the missis asked her to leave the door ajar so as to let the breeze blow in. When the house was quiet the missis fell asleep with the baby on her arm. Bye-and-bye she awoke all in a tremble, and there, squatted on the rafters above her head was Peter. He was looking down at her, pointing to baby, grinning and chattering, and making his red hair twitch up and down.

The missis folded the baby in her arms, too frightened to stir. Then Peter twisted his legs around the rafter and lowered himself down, pointing to baby and chattering as if pleased. The missis could bear it no longer; she managed to get the hair-brush off the table, and when next the boy lowered his ugly face she started up and gave him a good smack on the cheek. With a fierce yell he swung himself to the floor and was away. Mrs. Barton seeing him dart out, came running over, and there lay my poor missis as white as a sheet in a dead faint.

"A couple of nights after this, just about midnight, I was awakened by the missis calling out in a queer and shaky voice,

"Harry, Harry, I can't find baby!'

"Nonsense,' says I, 'she's rolled up in the blankets somewhere.'

"No, no,' says the wife, fairly crying now, 'she's not; oh, do get up, Harry.'

"I struck a match, then got up and searched. All through the house we looked, me and the missis, she, poor thing, crying and shaking all over; into every corner and crevice, but no use—the baby was gone. It was very strange. A baby of a few days old couldn't have unlocked the door, and it wasn't likely to have slipped out of bed and hidden itself just to aggravate you, as some of those youngsters will do, and its wonderful how soon they begin.

Sure enough the baby was gone, and it was not long before we had found out who had taken her and how he had made his way into the house. While searching around the place, I suddenly noticed that the fire-place was half-full of soot, and says I to myself, 'Peter has carried her off, and there's the way he got in.' It was easy enough for an ape like him to clamber up the wide chimney, made of wattle and dab, even with the baby.

QUEER!

For he could hold things under that stump as firm and fast as in a vice and have the good arm left for climbing.

The missus was nearly mad when I told her. She began to scream and cry out 'that her pretty baby was killed.' This woke up the other children. They began to howl, and there was me flying round from one to the other, and such a scene you never saw. If I could have put my hands on Peter I'd have throttled him there and then! Well, I started to go over to Barton's to tell them what was up, but as soon as I got outside the first thing I saw in the moonlight was the boy sitting down by the creek, nursing baby.

He was holding her quite comfortably in his one arm, soothing her and yabbering softly, while the baby, poor thing, was crying her very life out. I tried to steal up quietly, but that boy had ears as sharp as a cat's, and when he saw me coming he was off. He hobbled away across the creek, and went as fast on his lame legs as you would on your sound ones, off towards the town.

I went to Barton's, and it was plain enough how Peter had made his way out, for there was the big window at the end of the house wide open. I roused Barton up, and he said we had better wait awhile; Peter, he was sure, would bring back the baby all safe and sound in the morning. But I knew my missis couldn't and wouldn't wait, and I myself did not much like the idea of our pretty child being all night in that brute's arms. So we started off, and as we came to the township we heard a soft 'yabber, yabber' going on, and knew the pair were close to us.

We walked as quietly as could be, but Peter either saw or heard us, for the noise ceased. I was real mad by this time, and, stooping down, picked up a stone. Presently out from behind a pile of wood crept the boy, and I never saw him look half so horrible as he did that night. His flat, ugly face reeping cunningly round from between his shoulders, his sound arm holding baby, who was quiet, and the stump of an arm going up and down. He saw me and was making off, but I thought I might stop him with the stone. I didn't mean to kill him, poor mortal, but I did think I'd may be lame him. Well, I threw the stone, and hit him right in the middle of the back. The wild, shrill yell he gave made my blood run cold, and, thinks I, 'I've done for baby now; he'll kill her as sure as fate,' for he was off again full split towards the river.

The yell brought Barton round from the back of the house, and we ran on together. I never told him about the stone—I never dared to. It is a good mile to the river, and in those days you could get a fair run across the plain, so we were gaining on Peter fast, but when we came to the river he ran right up to the top of the 'Milestone,' and there, on the top of that big hillock of rock and earth, he stood grinning and dancing like a devil, and holding the poor baby in his one hand just over the deep, dark water where the Mataura sweeps round the base of the 'Milestone.' We didn't know what to do.

At last we made it up that Barton was to climb up one side of the mound and I the other, and try to take Peter by surprise. But when we got to the top there was nothing! Shaking all over I looked down into the deep pool, expecting to see the baby's white night dress floating there, but not a break was on the black water.

We searched all round and over the 'Milestone,' and about the place, but not a trace of either could we find. Well, we had to go home at last, and then there was a scene. Oh Lord!—I can't describe it. You married men may imagine, but you that are bachelors can't fancy nothing like it till you do get married—so there.

Harry paused and wiped his face with a red bandana, while Archie Black, as kind a fellow as ever walked, said,

'Have another drink, old son?'

"Well, Archie, I don't mind if I do." That recruited Harry, and he continued "Early next morning, Barton I, and half the men in the place started down the flat. We looked and searched everywhere, till after nightfall, but not a trace could we find.

Next day, however, Mrs. Barton made a strange discovery. The big window had been left open in the hope of Peter coming home, and when they got up in the morning an old feeding bottle that she kept over the mantel-piece, and with which Peter was very fond of playing, was gone. And when the goats were brought home that evening they were all milked dry! She hurried over to our place, and says she to my missis,

'Look here, Mrs. Clare, that baby of yours is just as safe as can be. Peter will bring her home all right, you mark me.'

"But the wife wouldn't be satisfied; she did not like the idea of that idiot for a wet nurse to her baby.

"Well, Peter hid himself securely, for our searchings were fruitless, but every evening the goats were milked, and every night a lot of bread and meat that Mrs. Barton left outside was taken except on the evenings when we kept watch about the house; then master Peter, with an idiot's cunning, kept out of the way.

One day I hit upon a plan, and this was it—to go away and watch by myself. So about midnight I set off, and kept on the spur opposite the 'Milestone.' All night I, by the bright spur watched and saw nothing; but just about dawn I made out a dark figure moving cautiously along the spur that joins the 'Milestone.' At once I knew it was Peter on his way to the town for supplies. As soon as he was out of sight I went over to the 'Milestone,' climbed to the top, and hid amongst the bushes. It was bright and clear, although the sun was not up, when I saw Peter returning, following a 'race' that runs along the spur. He was carrying a bundle of something under the stump, and a 'billy' in his hand. He came on steadily, then all of a sudden was gone. But the secret was out. I knew that there was a deserted 'drive' up on the spur, the more fool I for not remembering sooner, and there they must be hidden—Peter at any rate—and I was wild to know whether the baby was there too, alive or dead. But I had to wait for another twenty-four hours, for Peter would not stir out again that day. So I went home, but I never let on to the missis, for, bless you, she'd have gone off there and then, and would have fought the boy, tooth and nail, till she got her baby. You can't teach a woman caution; they don't understand the thing.

Away I went about three o'clock next morning, and had to wait an hour and a-half before Peter showed up. After he got well away I ran up the spur and into the tunnel. I pushed along; then it got dark, so I struck a match, lit a bit of candle I had brought in my pocket, and hurried on. And there, at the end of the drive, on a bed made of some torn-up grass and fern, covered with a couple of bags and some old clothes, lay the baby fast asleep, and smiling as natural as possible, with its thumb in its mouth. I caught it up, and before another hour the youngster was safe in her mother's arms, and the missis crying over it worse than the night it was lost. It's strange the way that women have; they cry when they are sorry, and they cry worse when they are glad. I can't make it out, but then there's a deal to understand about a woman.

When Peter found the baby was gone he came home as quiet as a lamb. But he couldn't be kept away from our place—morning, noon, and night he was prowling round. So the missis had the windows barred up, and the door with a new lock, and at night a blessed great heavy door sort of a thing up on the top of the chimney. I used sometimes to forget it when I was lighting the fire in the morning, and nearly smothered the family with smoke before they were out of bed. Well, everything went on all right. Barton used to make sure that Peter was well secured at night, and in the day time he used often to come over and sit in front of our door, moaning and crying like, but yabbering away jolly enough when he caught a sight of baby.

"Something turned up that I had to go away from home for a day or two, and of course, if any evil is going to happen, that's the time it will come. The very night I left, the missis was putting the youngsters to bed, baby was asleep in the inside room, one of the children was already undressed, and the other was playing and kicking as its mother took off its clothes, when it managed to knock the candle down, which rolled under the bed; in a moment the valance was in a blaze, and before the missis could open the front door and get water the partition was alight. It was only front door and get water the partition was alight. It was only made of scrim and a bit of paper, so it burned like tinder. Before the poor missis in her fright and confusion had the door unlocked the thatch had caught. She dragged one child out, and was just in time to save the other when all the lower end of the house was blazing. Poor thing! she was like one mad. The neighbours came running, but before they could even get across the creek, the baby, who was asleep in the bedroom near the partition, would be roasted. She dashed into the fire, but the fierce flames drove her back, with her hair singed and her clothes burning. Suddenly a strong arm pulled her back, and as she fell she saw Peter rush past her into the flames. The men were at the house now, and there, standing at the window, tearing away the fastenings with his one hand, while under the stump he held the baby, yelling wildly at the flames close behind, was Peter. At last the window gave way and he handed baby out gently and tenderly, but dropped down himself. The men got on the roof, tore away the thatch, called to Peter to get up and be pulled out, but he never stirred. The heat was too fierce to be borne, so the men had to jump down to save their lives.

In two hours' time nothing was left but a chimney, a few blackened poles, and a halfcharred shapeless mass, that every one feared to look at. But when all that remained of Barton's poor idiot was placed in the coffin, and my missis went to look at him for the last time, she cried as bitterly as if he had been her own.'

A MEMBER OF THE FORCE

"Come now, Archie, it's your turn for a story?" said Jack Conliffe.

Archie only turned his big form in closer proximity to the fire and, laughingly, replied:

"Well, you see, boys, I know nothing of babies either from practice or precept, and as all your yarns to-night have been about youngsters, and I can't follow suit, and it is too late to play a new lead—so I'll shout."

"That you won't," said Harry Clare, "I've told my story, and now I'm going to stand treat; you've shouted for us already, so now you tell a yarn."

"Weren't you with that Sergeant who was drowned in the Waikaia over on Switzers side?" asked Jack. "Tell us about that. What was his name to begin with?"

"His name was Michael Brennan, and he was as fine a fellow as ever walked, although he was 'a bobby.' He used to have to visit Nokomai, so may be some of you boys have seen him."

"No!" "Well, he was a bigger man than me, and taller, with black hair and whiskers, and big dark eyes, a real jolly fellow as ever I came across. There was never a dance or a spree but Brennan was sure to be in it. Of course he had to take his fun quietly because of his billet, but he did have lots of jollity for all that. But there was one good thing about him, he did not drink. I don't mean that he was teetotal, you know—he would have his nip like any other man—but he only got real tight twice in all the time I knew him. Once was the first night he came to Switzers, and of course no one took any notice of that. The other time you will hear about before I've finished my yarn. I don't think any of you boys were at Switzers when Frenchman's Hill was going a-head.

What, you have never been in Switzers at all! Well, it's not much of a place to look at now, for the gold has pretty well run out; but, my word, it was a rare rowdy quarter in '66 or thereabouts. The township is planted right on the top of a steep spur; you must climb a hill to get at it on any side. And then it is almost an island, the Winding Creek being on one side, and the Waikaia River a little further off on the other. When I first saw it there must have been close on 2,000 men working about, and the whole top of the hill was covered with houses just as close as they could stick, most of them of canvass and roofed with zinc, and nearly every second house was a 'shanty' or a store. There was drinking and dancing, shouting and billiard-playing every night from dark till daylight. Everybody was making money and every body spent it. I often sold my gold for £50 on Saturday, and on Monday had not a five pound note. Ah! those were rare old times! I don't think though that any of the boys made much out of it, though the 'shanties' cleared their hundreds a week. I don't know how old Brennan stood it, for he was always in the thick of the fun, and I suppose he only had his fixed wages to go upon.

Well, at this time I was mates with a young fellow called Jim Smith, a good enough lad as a mate, and would do just as big a day's labour as any man, but an awful chap for a rowdy spree, and when he was drunk he was an out-and-out scoundrel. Poor lad, he was my mate, but what I've said is only the truth about him. The Crown Hotel in Switzers had a bar-maid at the time—a regular plum, the boys were all just mad about her. A little thing she was, but with the prettiest of round faces and brown hair, and the most bewitching eyes, and she used to throw a glance of them at a fellow and it was all over with him. What do you say, Jack? 'You suppose I was smitten too.' Of course I was,

I never could resist a pretty woman, and no man living could withstand one arch look from Lily's brown eyes. But she had completely captivated the Sergeant and my mate. I don't believe she cared a bit for Jim, only she liked to flirt with him when no one else was handy; but with the Sergeant it was different. She would be as demure as possible when he was near her and you couldn't get a word of fun or chaff from her.

Old Brennan just worshipped her, but he was a fool, for he thought Lily only cared for him, while everyone else knew she never was happy without half-a-dozen followers, and would string men on with mischievous glances and pretty words, and squeezings of her warm little hands, just for the fun of laughing at them.

Well, one Saturday evening, Jim and I went down to the township. At this time we were working at a place called 'Gow's Creek,' over the river up among the hills, but we generally went to Switzers every fortnight or so to sell our gold and get stores.

Of course we could not dream of going home without calling on Lily. So, going to The Crown Hotel we made at once for the little back parlour, sacred to Lily and her special friends. There was the little girl looking as neat and as pretty as a flower. I think that was Lily's greatest charm; she was always neat—her dress seemed better made than those of the other women, and the colours always blended nicely and tastefully. But here too we found the Sergeant, seemingly quite at home. I was glad to see him, but Jim looked as black as thunder, and was for going away. However, Lily would not have that; she came to him with both hands out, and her big eyes looking so pleadingly into his face.'

'Ah, Jim, don't go away. I've been wondering so that you haven't been to see me. I was beginning to think you didn't care to come. There, now, I will give you my own arm chair, and that I wouldn't do for any one else'—'Except you,' she whispered to the Sergeant, who was handing her a chair. I heard the aside, although it was spoken low. The Sergeant and I now were together, and trying to make conversation, but I could scarcely help smiling to see him glancing every minute at Lily, who sat with her little feet up on the hob talking away merrily to Jim.

"'Really, Jim, I was quite angry to think you never came to see me when last you were down. You didn't know how much I missed you.'

"'I don't think you can miss any one much,' said Jim, moodily, 'you seem to have plenty of friends always about.'

"'I don't know what you mean. I have not nearly enough friends. What do you mean? tell me, Jim?'

Jim chose to whisper his reply, a most convenient way, I thought, as he drew her pretty face so close to his own. Then Jim must needs admire her bracelet, and of course, had to hold her hand in his while examining the trinket. Perhaps the Sergeant thought the examination was lasting too long, for he called for 'drinks,' which necessitated Lily's rising to give the message to the barman. Then the Sergeant quietly slipped into her place and engaged Jim in some discussion about the price of gold.

When Lily came back she took the vacant seat. Jim tried to right affairs by reminding the Sergeant of the change, but Lily merely said, 'Oh, never mind, Sergeant, I would just as soon sit here,' and forthwith began to talk to me, but every now and then darting a smiling, loving glance at Jim.

However, the evening passed away very fairly; the Sergeant told Irish stories with a brogue and a wittiness that even Jim had to laugh in spite of himself, and he sung jovial songs in which we all joined in chorus whether we knew the tune or not. But at last, as bad luck would have it, Brennan pitched on 'Molly Asthore,' and put his whole heart into the song, singing at and for Lily alone, as every one could see, while that young lady made eyes at him and blushed and simpered just as conscious and as pleased as could be.

Now, I don't wonder poor Jim was angry; it is hard lines to

have to sit and listen to a big handsome fellow singing soft songs to the girl you like best, and that too with a voice that would charm the heart of a nun. But for all that, Jim need not have been such a fool as to sneer and mutter something about 'a blathering Irish idiot.' Brennan's face grew as black as thunder, but Lily patted his shoulder and said, 'O thank you, Sergeant, such a lovely song. Now there's no use in any one trying to sing again after that, so we'll have a game of whist, and you must be my partner, Jim.' Then she drew a chair quite close, settled herself down cosily, and said, smiling up into Jim's face—'Do you know, Jim, you are the only good partner I ever get—I wish I had you always.'

'Upon my word!' laughed the Sergeant, 'I wonder is this leap year?' Then Lily got quite confused, and said she did not mean anything at all, and did not know how she could have been so stupid, and it was hard to tell whose face was the reddest, hers or Jim's. But in spite of his pretty partner Jim managed to lose every game. Perhaps it was her fault, for she wouldn't attend to what was going on, but must needs be giving sly glances at the Sergeant, and making little signals to him.

At last, when she was pretending to show him all her cards, Jim flung down his 'hand,' and with a thump of his fist on the table, swore he wouldn't play any longer with a couple of cheats.

Up jumped Brennan, seized Jim by the collar, and dragged him into the middle of the room. I tried to interfere, but one push of the Sergeant's strong arm sent me flying. Then he said, speaking quite coolly and deliberately, 'Now, my friend Mr. Smith, that last remark of yours could only be meant either for me or the lady I was talking to; if it was for me, I'll punch your head; if it was for her, I'll break your ugly neck: now, speak out.'

Jim could not do more than struggle in the Sergeant's grasp, but if ever a man's thoughts were told in a look, Jim's face spoke 'murder' as plain as words. However, to our great surprise, my mate suddenly turned quite polite and said 'I beg your pardon, Mr. Brennan, and I am very sorry for the remark. I was angry, and did not mean it for anyone. Come, forget it, and let us have a drink.'

"'It's a good thing for your hide you have apologised,' said the Sergeant, 'but as for the rest, I drink with honest men, and not with a liar and a coward.'

Jim's face turned white at the words, but he only said, 'Oh, well, please yourself, I'm off to bed.' Of course that put an end to our pleasant evening. Lily had run away at the first symptoms of a row, and after a good-night 'nip,' the Sergeant left for the camp.

Of course I thought Jim would clear out early next morning, but he didn't show up until after breakfast, and then went went straight off to the Camp, of all places in the world. I suppose he and the Sergeant made the quarrel up in some way, for he told us Brennan had promised to come up in the evening. Well, I never did think much of my mate as a man, but before I'd go and eat humble pie to the Sergeant or any other man he might break my neck, if I wasn't able first to settle him.

Well, the Sergeant did not come until late, after ten o'clock, and we all, that is, he, Jim, Lily, and I, gathered in the little parlour. But it wasn't comfortable. Lily was as quiet as a mouse, keeping an anxious eye on Brennan and Jim, and of course, after what had happened the night before, one daren't even mention cards. So we talked a little, and had several drinks, till Lily said she was tired and must go to bed. Then the landlord closed the house and came to join us by the fire. After a little he asked us what we were going to have, and the Sergeant, I remember, took some cordial—cloves, I think.

"'Don't disturb yourself, boss,' said Jim, as the landlord was about to get up, 'Ill get the drinks.'

Jim knew the bar well, and as the boss was stout and not very active, he was ready enough to sit still in his easy chair. Jim was so long over his work that when he did come back the landlord said:

"'Well, I began to think as you must have been brewing fresh beer for us, Jim?'

"'Oh, dash it all?' said Jim, 'you've altered the bar since I was down last, and I couldn't put my hand on a thing.' "When we had finished our drinks, Brennan exclaimed—

"'I say, boss, that's infernally bad stuff of yours, it is making me quite sick."

"'Right you are, Brennan,' put in Jim, 'it is bad stuff, I had a nip of it this morning and it nearly killed me. You'd better take a drop of something strong to keep off bad effects.'

"'Faith, I think you're right, Jim, I'll have a nip of whisky.'

"'Oh, by jove! Sergeant, the whisky is worse than the other—try some rum.'

"'All right, Jim, please yourself'

"This last supply of drinks had a very queer effect on Brennan.

When he first came in he had been very gloomy and cross, but suddenly became quite jolly, laughing at nothing at all, singing song after song and telling all sorts of funny yarns. Of course there were two or three more 'shouts,' and at last I thought old Brennan was fairly going mad. The landlord tried to get us to bed, but the Sergeant would not hear of it, and Jim kept backing him up. At last Jim found a Jew's harp lying on the mantelpiece and began to tinkle out an Irish jig tune. Up got the Sergeant, and though he could not stand straight, he must try to dance. Of course he fell, right across the little table and smashed it down. But he was on his feet in a minute, seized a leg of the table that was hanging loose, and commenced to flourish it round his head with a wild 'Hurroo!'

"'Go it, your sowl,' shouted Jim. The Sergeant let fly at the mantelpiece, and crash went the vases and the big looking-glass on the wall above it. Then he rushed out into the bar, and in a very few minutes the place was strewn with broken glass, and pools of liquor flooded the floor. Next he went off into the passage, where, fortunately, the front door was locked. Jim followed him close, there was a slight scuffle, then a heavy fall, and when we got out, Brennan lay insensible, bleeding from a severe scalp wound. Jim said he had struck against the door handle in his fall.

We got him to bed, where he slept motionless till late next day. Then he awoke to find his head all bandaged up, and the unpleasant memory of the last night's row. But when he knew all the damage he had done, he was in an awful state of mind. He sent for the landlord, and, of course, had to pay all breakages, and one way or another that spree couldn't have cost less than £25. But it was not so much the money he minded as the fear that some report would get to the ears of the Inspector of Police. Fortunately, there were only few persons present; the boss was glad to be quiet for the credit of his house, and I thought I might safely promise both for Jim and myself. Jim cleared out for home early next morning, and Brennan did not see him again.

Just before I left for home, Lily said she wanted to speak to me particularly, so we went into her private parlour and she locked the door.

"'Wasn't it a strange thing the way the poor sergeant got on the other evening?' she asked.

"I said it was the strangest thing I had ever seen. He had taken only three or four glasses when he was mad drunk.

"'Oh! it couldn't have been the quantity!' said the girl, 'I have known him to take a dozen 'nips' in an evening without being the least the worse of it. No, Archie, it wasn't the quantity.'

"'Well, but what was it then?' asked I.

"'Will you promise not to be offended if I tell you something strange about your mate?'

I told her she might say what she pleased about Jim so far as I was concerned.

"'Well, Archie, after I left you that evening I went to my bedroom; but I had some sewing to do, and as there was a good fire in the kitchen I went in there. By-and-bye I wanted my scissors, and remembered they were lying in the parlour just opposite to this. I had a pair of old slippers on and came very quietly along the passage, but on opening the door of the parlour, to my surprise there was Jim. He had a tray of glasses, and was bending over them, but I could not see that he was doing anything more, only he put his hand into his pocket all of a sudden.'

"'Well, Lily, and what more? Do you think Jim was doing anything with the drink?'

"'Yes, I do, there, that's plain enough. I think he was putting some doctor's stuff in them to make Brennan tight.'

"'Lily, my girl,' said I, 'that is a very serious thing to say against a man. I never did think Jim an extra good fellow, but I doubt if he is blackguard enough for that.'

"'Oh! isn't he? Well, he is blackguard enough to go about the place whispering nasty stories about me and the Sergeant, and a man that is mean enough for that will do anything, I think.'

"'Yes, you are right enough there, Lil, but I don't like this poisoning idea.'

"'Why should not a man murder another with poison as well as any other way?'

"'But you surely do not think Jim would murder Brennan?'

"'Yes, I do, if only he could do it safely.'

"'Lily, Lily, I wonder if you would say this if any other man than the Sergeant was hurt?'

"'Yes, of course I would. Oh, I know what you mean, Archie, and at any rate I will say I like the Sergeant fifty thousand times better than a sneaking, murdering villain like Jim Smith.'

"'That's right, Lily, don't spare him.'

"'Wait till you hear the rest that I have to tell before you know if he deserves to be spared. You know the Sergeant says now that when he fell in the passage, he did not hit his head against the door, but that some one struck him with a stick.'

"'Ah, but, poor old fellow, he was too far gone to be certain of anything that happened that night.'

"'Perhaps so, but wait a little. Yesterday morning, one of the girls was sick, and I had to help to do up the rooms. I got the room that Jim had slept in—perhaps I took it on purpose, but never mind. At any rate, I took the chance to examine it well. I thought he might forget and leave some bottles of his poisons about. I didn't have the luck to find one of them, but I'll show you what I did get.'

"She produced from behind her table, a walking stick with a white bone handle, on which there was an ugly dark stain. It was a weapon that could be made to give a very nasty blow.'—'And,' Lily continued, 'he had it so cunningly thrust away underneath the chest of drawers. It is the boss's walking stick, and always used to hang in the passage, just a handy place for Jim to get it that night. And look at that stain; what did that, do you think? No, of course it never was there before, nor would be now, only Jim thought he could knock the Sergeant's life out with it. What do you think of your mate now, Archie?'

"'I think he's a low, bad scoundrel, Lily; but what are you going to do with the stick?'

"'Why, I am going to show it to the boss, and see if I can't get that brute punished as he ought to be.'

"'Well, you will be foolish if you do, Lil. You see there is no proof that Jim either 'hocussed' the Sergeant's drink, or used the stick to hurt him.'

"'Why, what proof more is wanted?' said Lily, indignantly, "doesn't everyone know that Jim hates poor Brennan like poison. See the way he looks at him with murder in his eyes? I don't want any more proof; I'm sure that Jim tried to murder the poor man; I'm sure of it.'

"'But how can you prove it, Lil? Jim might say that the stick was in the bedroom before he came there at all, and as for the poor old Sergeant's assertion, about not striking his head, I'm afraid his word would go for very little, considering the state he was in that night.'

"'Oh,' rejoined Lily, with a toss of her pretty head, 'of course you stick up for your mate, but I'm sure he did it on purpose.'

"'But why are you sure?'

"'Oh because—because, well, just because I am.'

"It is hard to reason with a woman, you know, boys; once let them get a thing into their heads and they'll stick to it right or wrong. So I said:

"'Well, perhaps you are right, Lily; but look here, supposing you go and speak to the boss about your suspicions, there will sure to be an enquiry into the affair, and what will become of poor Brennan? It will be hard enough for him to clear himself as it is, and if all the facts of the case came out he would lose his billet to a certainty.'

This idea seemed to frighten the girl. She stood awhile, taping her pretty foot impatiently on the ground, then went off saying—

"'Well, I don't care what anyone thinks, I'm sure Jim Smith tried to murder the Sergeant that night. I'm sure of it, so there now.'

Still, I thought she would keep quiet for fear of injuring the man she was so fond of, and I was right. I cleared out for home next day, and found Jim very sulky, but not one word passed between us as to the 'set to' in the town. There was one thing good about Jim (and even this was not of his own nature) he had received an excellent schooling. He could write like copperplate and spell like a dictionary. Every evening, for the first few days after our return, he was writing letters, or, rather, writing one letter over and over again, and then seeing something wrong about it and tearing it up. This went on till at last I said:

"'That must be a mighty particular letter of yours, Jim, for you've wrote it over a dozen times. Is it a gushing love-letter?'

He looked, and laughing unpleasantly, said:

"'Yes, you're right, Archie, it is a love-letter.'

He seemed to be satisfied with the epistle he concocted that night, and took it to the post next day. Well, it might have been a fortnight after this when I happened to be alone in the hut one afternoon, and to my surprise who should ride up but the Inspector of Police. I had seen him before once or twice in the township. He soon began asking me questions about the Sergeant, whether I was well acquainted with him, and what sort of a character he bore in the town; whether he was a general of a character he bore in the town; whether he was a general favourite there or not. I said I thought not, as he was too severe to be much liked. Then a few more 'hums-and-haws,' for the fellow was a mighty 'haw-haw' individual, but not one word about the particular row in the Hotel.

By-and-bye, he asked for my mate. I said he was away from home—and so he was, a couple of hundred yards away, "working in the claim, but that I not think necessary to explain. So very soon, my gentleman rode off, and I blest my stars that he was gone before Jim put in an appearance. Jim had not seen him come or go. I did not tell him, for somehow I had a misgiving that if he knew, he would be off to the town and then would tell enough to ruin the poor old Sergeant.

As it was poor Brennan came in for it, for in some way the Inspector had got hold of a mild account of the affair, but what he did hear was enough to get the Sergeant a severe lecturing, as well as to be reduced to the rank of constable, and lose his stripes. It was hard lines on him, poor fellow, but bless you, those that were fond of him liked him just as well with stripes or without. Somehow the notion arose in the town that Jim Smith had sent in the report which caused old Brennan to be disgraced—none of us had any proof of it, but, Lily like, we were sure for all that.

SECOND PART.

"Well," said Archie, resuming his story, "things went on very quietly after this till Christmas time drew near. Jim and I were working steadily, intending to wash up just before the holidays, and then go into the township for a spree. The winter had been a severe one, and the spring unusually late and cold, so that even in the beginning of December the higher ranges were still covered with snow. But summer came at last with a rush. Days so hot that one could scarcely live after the bracing cold weather we had been having, and warm soft winds blowing that sent the rivers and creeks up and kept them high. Jim and I were rejoicing over such plenty of water, and thinking what a good washing up we would have, when our proceedings came to a sudden stop in a way we little looked for.

We went to work as usual one morning; I was down in the tail-race, and Jim working just under the face. We had been there perhaps a couple of hours, when all of a sudden I was startled by a loud sharp yell from him. I knew that something bad had happened, but, good Lord, boys, it was a terrible sight I saw when I reached him. A big boulder had slipped from the face, and striking right him right between the shoulders, had pinned him to the ground No, he wasn't dead, better for the poor chap if he had been for I'll never forget to my dying day the awful look; of his white face, half turned round from under the big stone, and one hand tearing in agony at the grass by his side.

It took all my strength with the help of a lever to shift away the stone, and his moaning and crying made me as weak as water and then how to get him home I didn't know, for there wasn't a soul to get help from nearer than the town.

At last some way or another I put him into the barrow, wheeled him home as gently as I could, and got him on to his bunk. I made him as comfortable as possible with pillows and blankets doubled up, and then there was nothing for it but to ride away to the township for the doctor. It did seem cruel to leave the poor fellow there, all smashed and hurt so badly, but what could I do? There wasn't even so much as a drop of brandy in the hut to give him, so I caught my moke, and, though I never rode so fast before, it was late when I reached "The Hill," and the rain that had been threatening all day was then falling steadily, and after all my hurry I was sold, for the doctor had been called away to a bad case at some of the stations, and no one knew when he would be back. Of course it wouldn't do to wait and let poor Jim die meantime, so I went to a chemist fellow that had a bit of a shop, and told him all that had happened. He said there was little he could do, but he gave me a lotion, and then says he,

'If your mate has any of that drug left he got here a few weeks ago it might be as well to give him a grain or two to make him sleep, but be careful, for it is very powerful.'

Said I, 'I won't go meddling with no drugs, just you make up the right amount yourself, and I'll give it to him;' but I began then to fear that Lily's suspicions were only too true.

When the medicine was ready and I came out of the Shop, first thing I saw in the street was the Sergeant's big chesnut horse, tied to the post in front of The Crown Hotel. So I thought I would go in and tell him about the accident. He had just come home from a long ride, having been to bring the escort down from Nokomai. He was sitting in Lily's room, comfortably ensconced blazing fire, and that young lady on the hearth-rug at his feet. And she did look killing, I tell you, with her black silk dress with crimson bow at the neck, and crimson velvet in her shiny hair, and the firelight dancing on her upturned face, with its big brown eyes, and her slender fingers clasped upon her lap. Oh, Lord! Oh, Lord! I'm growing quiet poetical as I think of it, so boss, hurry up and bring us some more 'nips.'

The 'nips' satisfactorily dispatched, Archie went on with his tale.

"Well, I found the sergeant had heard of the accident, and he said to me,

"'When do you start back, Archie?'

"'Now, at once,' says I.

"'Well just wait till I get a nip and a handful of biscuits, and I'll go with you. I'm afraid no one can do much for him, but it won't do to let him die there alone.'

"'Ah! now, Sergeant,' cried Lily, with a pout that made her look prettier than ever, 'Here you've been away three days, and now you are off again, and for a man that would—well, never mind, he is no friend of yours, to say the least of it.'

"'Lily, my girl,' said he gravely, 'friend or not has nothing to do with it. I must go, and will, so you'll get me a handful of biscuits and fill this flask with P.B., and be quick, my dear. I do wish I could get a feed for the old moke, but he must just make the best of it.'

Lily got the things, and just as we were starting she called me back, and shutting the door, says in a soft voice, 'Archie, do you think Jim is very badly hurt?'

"'I do, indeed, as bad as can be almost.'

"'Oh, poor fellow, poor fellow,' she said, with her sweet voice all a tremble and her eyes quite dim; 'you'll tell him, Archie, I am so very sorry, please,' and she looked so tender and kind and pitiful, that I just felt like taking her in my arms and giving her a good kiss there and then.

"And may be you didn't do it, too?" said one of the listeners in a suggestive voice.

"'Never you mind,' retorted Achie, 'that's got nothing to do with the yarn.'

"The Sergeant was already on his horse, a regular brute, that plunged and reared, and at last tried a bit of bucking before he would be turned away from home.

"'Now mind, sergeant,' cried Lily as we started, 'you've promised that you will be here for the Christmas dinner the lay after to-morrow, and nothing is to present you.'

"'All right Lily, sweetheart, nothing shall prevent me; but if you, don't give me plenty of goose and apple sauce I'll never kiss you again.'

"'Well, I'm sure!' exclaimed the lady, blushing all over her pretty face, 'the impudence of you men! I think, indeed, you are goose enough already.'

"'So I am, my dear, and you are my apple sauce,' called out the jolly Sergeant as we rode away.

It was a terrible evening to be out. For all it was summer time, sharp breezes came sweeping off the lofty hills which we were nearing every half-hour, and a soft, steady rain was falling, that soaked us to the skin. Neither of our horses was very fresh, and this made the ride more tiresome. We did not reach the hut till after ten o'clock. Taking the saddles from our horses, we let them go. The sergeant said he could trust the chestnut, while my horse of coarse was at home. A cold shiver came over me as we got close to the dark, silent hut, for I could not help wondering whether we should find Jim stiff and cold or still alive, and it was a queer thing, but it was the dead Jim that I was frightened of.

But when we pushed open the door we heard a low moan, and knew that he was able to suffer still. We soon had a light, and there lay poor Jim, just as I had left him, but with his eyes shut and his senses gone with the pain. We had first to try and strip him, and, do you know, it was wonderful to see how tenderly Brennan handled him. When I tried, my awkward touch made him yell and cry, but the big Sergeant moved him as gently as a woman could, and he never made more than a moan. I soon had a good fire alight, and in less than no time Brennan had some of our beef cut lip and stewing for beef tea, and had given Jim a nip and then the draught, and he was fast asleep.

The Sergeant said, 'I don't think he's dangerously hurt, Archie, but I'm afraid he will have to suffer a lot yet. I wish to Heaven the doctor was here.'

By and by Brennan turned in to my bunk, for he was fairly tired out, and I was to watch the patient.

Jim slept quietly till nearly morning, when he began to moan and stir uneasily, and by and by woke with a terrible shriek that roused Brennan, who said, 'Ah! this was what I feared; he's delirious.'

"All that day he raved and cried like a madman, and didn't know who either of us was. All of a sudden he seemed to take me for the chemist, and said he wanted to buy so drug; then he lay still awhile, muttering to himself very low. But at last he whispers, 'Ah! this is the brute's glass—there—that will make him tight enough, the -Irish fool, and you will know him, Lily, my girl.'

"Then for a little while he lay quiet, then called out, 'Sergeant! Sergeant!" in a voice so natural that I was certain he knew Brennan, who was seated behind him and holding him up. But Jim was only raving, for he went on, 'I say, Sergeant, I nearly finished you that night. The drink nearly cooked you, and if your head hadn't been as hard as granite that rap would have settled you. The stick—where is it? Ah! take it away, Archie—burn it! burn it! See! it has blood upon it—the Sergeant's blood! Burn it, Archie! Quick—here's Lily coming—quick, quick."

"And so he raved on half the day, confessing all his villainy, while poor Brennan had to listen, but his face was as red as if he were overhearing something he ought not to. But he never left Jim, bathing his forehead with vinegar and giving him nips of brandy, while Jim mistook him sometimes for me, sometimes for a stranger, and at last for his own father, and begged him to pray God to save him from being hanged, with cries and wild words pitiful to hear. We gave him his sleeping draught, but it seemed rather to make him worse than better, till at last, in despair, the Sergeant began to sing. I suppose it was thinking of the sad state the poor fellow was in, and the near approach of Christmas time, but it was a hymn he chose, one that I have heard my mother sing a score of times, about the 'shepherds that were watching their flocks by night, all seated on the ground.' The Sergeant sang very low and sweetly, with a curious tremble in his voice I never noticed before. The song quieted and soothed Jim wonderfully, and as for me I just sat looking out through the open door, till the dreary grey flat, with the heavy sky raining over it, faded quite away, and I was back again in the old home place, and could see the cosy old red brick farm-house, with its shingled roof, the big gum trees beside the gate, the honeysuckle round the windows, and my old mother a-sitting at the door in the twilight singing to us youngsters before we went to bed.

Well, well, anyhow before the hymn was done poor Jim was sleeping like a child, and holding the Sergeant's hand fast in his own. He slept for hours, and the Sergeant managed to slip away, while I took his place. When Jim awoke he was quite sensible, but in terrible agony. It was dreadful to listen to the poor fellow's low constant moaning. He recognized Brennan as soon as he saw him, but seemed to grow restless and nervous all the time he was in the hut, and when he went out Jim said, 'Archie, for God's sake get the doctor!'

"I told him I was afraid the river was now so high as to be impassable. When Brennan came in again Jim begged him to go for medical aid. The Sergeant hesitated, and said he did not like the look of the river.

"'What!' asked Jim, 'are you so much of a coward to be afraid to swim a river to get help for a dying man?'

Brennan's face got quite red at the thought of being called a coward, and he said, 'I'll go, Jim, at once. Come and give me a hand with the moke, Archie.'

When the horse was ready I told Jim I was going to see the

Sergeant cross the river, and would be back soon, so Brennan and I went down the flat. The river was an ugly sight to see. Flooded far beyond its banks, muddy and thick it came pouring down in a yellow swirling stream. About ten yards below the usual ford is a steep bank, and beneath it a deep pool; and in order to avoid this by landing above it Brennan selected a place about twenty yards higher to go in. The current would sweep the horse down, but he thought he could guide the animal so as to land on a spit upon the other side. The chestnut did not like the idea of going into the water; I suppose the poor brute's instinct told him there was danger. In he would not go. He plunged, reared, bucked, and shied till Brennan got fairly mad.

"'Archie' said he, 'go and break a big branch off one of the manukas, and if this devil don't go in next time let him have it hot and heavy.'

I got the branch, and the chestnut was tried again, but without success. Brennan sang out, and I came down with the manuka on the horse's back. He went in then. He gave such a jump that expected to see the Sergeant off into the river. But Brennan sat firm, keeping the horse well in hand, and now the chestnut finding himself fairly in for it, struck out gamely. The yellow bubbling water was above the saddle, round the Sergeant's waist, and he leant a little forward clapping the horse's neck and encouraging him. They had got perhaps a quarter of the way across when I caught sight of something that made me sick with fear. It was a big tree being swept down, and I saw that if the Sergeant did not keep a little farther down the river it would be borne right against him. I shouted, and Brennan tried to look round, but either he mistook my meaning or got confused, for he turned the horse's head straight across the river. On came the tree, rolling over and over with a fearful strength and speed. In one minute more it was bang! against the chestnut's ribs. The horse gave a shrill neigh, a wild struggle, and the next thing I knew, Brennan was off; and then I remembered that he could not swim a stroke. The house plunged, gasped, and turned over on his side. His ribs were broken by that terrible collision. Poor Brennan only struggled a minute, then the current swept him off, his arms waved wildly once or twice, and once I saw his face; and, boys, never till my dying day will I forget that awful last look.

I went away back to the station as hard as I could, and all the men there, the boss and all, turned out to search for poor old Mick. I must have been cranky at the time, for I forgot all about Jim, and only when we were on the point of starting did I remember. Then a lad from the station offered to go and look after him till we came back. We did not find Brennan for two days, and then a long way down the river. He was washed upon a sand bank, not bruised or discoloured. His one hand was under his head and his eyes closed, lying quite peaceable as if asleep; there was even something like a shadowy smile on his brave old face.

When the terrible news was told to Jim Smith, he said nothing, but only lay without speaking all day. Lily, they said, was heart broken, and cried her pretty face very red. Jim didn't die. The doctor said he had better be brought down to the township, and there were plenty of volunteers for bearers. He was carried to 'The Crown,' for there was then no hospital in Switzers. Lily seemed afraid of him at first, but gradually came to nurse him and attend to him more than any one. When Jim got able to move he went to Dunedin. Lily also went to town a short time after. But they came back together, and Lily Mrs. Jim Smith. I wasn't much surprised.

A woman can weep always for a first love when the second is young, Wood-looting, and well-to-do. She is a good little woman, and makes Jim Smith just as loving a wife as if she had never heard of such a person as Sergeant Michael Brennan."

THE PATER'S GHOST STORY.

It now came to my turn to tell some tale, and as everyone else had done their best willingly, I could not ask to be excused. So I said, "Well, boys, I am not a good hand at telling a story, but, if you like, I will read one that a friend once told to me."

As they were agreeable, I went to my bedroom and brought back with me a notebook, from which I read The "Pater's Ghost Story," as follows:—

"It was just the night for a story. The wind was loud and boisterous, now dying out in low sobs, now shrieking in wild glee, making the house tremble with its force, and we knew that if the warm green curtains at the windows were drawn aside we should see the snow-flakes swirling down ward through the gloom.

All this, however, only enhanced the comfort we felt in the good fire that brightened up the objects near at hand, but made strange shadows stir in the distant corners, and flicker, phantom-like, against the further walls. We were alone in the house, the Pater and I. My chair was tilted comfortably aslant, while he, with his arms folded behind his head, lay back in a low arm-chair. His two dogs, brown, curly-haired, wise-eyed retrievers, snoozed luxuriously at our feet. Presently a gust of unusual violence struck the house, and roared about the roof, renewed again and again with such wild clamour, that I exclaimed—'By Jove! Pater, isn't it an awful night!' Then I repeated, half-unconsciously, Robert Buchanan's weird lines beginning, The wind, lad, the wind, how it blows, how it blows, it gripes the latch, it shakes the house, it whistles, it screams, it crows!'

The Pater nodded assent, but spake no word. Let me here explain that, beyond a long and sincere friendship, there is no other connection between the Pater and myself—no tie of blood or birth, not even that slight link which makes men of the same country one kin. But long years passed close together have given to each a feeling of Action and esteem that time cannot destroy.

As to the nickname of 'Pater,' it was given to him in kindly recognition of many friendly deeds, of many pleasant hours passed together, of pranks we played, and cares or sorrows we have known; and the familiar by-name is now more commonly used between us than his own proper Patronymic. As his real name is of no consequence to this story, I have chosen the title 'Pater' to introduce as good a friend and as hearty a fellow as ever the sun shone on. So we sat together this evening, the Pater and I, silent for the most part—old friends have no need to keep up that distressing flow of small talk, which politeness demands among mere acquaintances.

For a time, no sound was audible but the roar and piping of the wind as it rose or died away, and the impolite snoring of the dogs at our feet. At length, when it seemed likely that we would follow the example of those wise animals, I said,

'Pater, rouse up and tell a story.' Now, the art of story-telling is one of the Pater's special accomplishments, and many a pleasant hour have I passed in listening to his gruesome Highland legends, his tales of 'suffering, want, and woe' in the Crimea; his reminiscences sounding like pages from 'The Arabian Nights'—of the ruined palaces or desolated shrines at Delhi and Lucknow, and his vivid descriptions of the life and scenery of that wondrous Oriental land. But to-night the Pater was lazy, protesting I had heard all his tales again and but finally relented so far as to ask what kind of story I wanted.

"'Oh! a good cold-blooded murder or a ghost story is most

fitting for a night like this.'

"'Well, as I have never committed a murder, nor yet have shuffled off this mortal coil, I don't see how I can easily suit you.'

"'Now, Pater, don't begin to attempt sharp answers, for you get very unpleasant in that way sometimes. Be obliging—just for a change, you know.'

"'Thanks for the compliment. But it is stupid to retail secondhand stories, and the only ghost I ever saw you must have heard of long ago, for the affair happened in this very township.'

"'The ghost you saw, and here! By Jove, that's glorious! I'll put on another log before you begin, for I might not be game to face the dark when you have finished.'

"So when I had replenished the fire, swung the kettle above the blaze, shaken the snowflakes from my coat and once more placed my chair comfortably aslant, I signified my readiness to listen by the familiar, if slangy, expression, 'Now then, Pater, go a-head.'

"'You must not look for anything too wonderful in this story of mine, Harry, nor can I tell why or wherefore it should have happened to me. It led to no ultimate discovery of murder or foul play, as ghostly visits are generally said to do. Only I am sure of this: That I saw clearly and distinctly all I am going to tell you, and that at the time I was neither drunk nor dreaming.'

"He paused, and I nodded to assure him of my acceptance of the conditions of his story, then drew my chair in closer to listen.

"Looking now to that evening, many years ago, fancy brings back the time, and again I am sitting in the red firelight, looking into the Pater's kindly face, brightened by expressive, keen, grey eyes, and hearing the slow, distinct, earnest voice that rose and fell, or at times paused awhile to give full effect to his tale, while, outside, the wind sobbed plaintively or rose to a fierce shriek, making this strange story seem yet more weird and awful.

"'You recollect,' continued the Pater, 'that accident which happened at Donnybrook when poor Ned Bolton was crushed by a fall of earth? Then, you know, there arose a dispute as to the actual cause of death, and it was decided to hold an inquest. Well, I left this place to carry the mail up to Nokomai the day previous to that on which Bolton died, and when I went from home he was not thought to be in any very great danger. Of course I remained that night at Nokomai, then had to go on to the Upper Nevis, so that four days elapsed before I returned. I got back here in the evening shortly after dark, put my horse in the stable, and went to light the lantern to bed him down. But I found the lantern had been moved, and as I knew there was some loose straw in the next stall, I thought I could do the work without the trouble of going for a light.

Groping about in the stall, I came suddenly against some strange object. It seemed to be ting on a tressel, and feeling still farther, I started back in instinctive horror when I recognised the stiff, cold, damp form as a human body. The shock was over in an instant, only the puzzle remained as to whom it could be, and why it was put in the stable I gathered up the straw, and without lighting the lantern, fed my horse and was ready to go.

"'And not unwilling, I should think, with that ghastly object close at hand, Pater?'

"'It made no difference, lad, nor would it necessarily have been 'a ghastly object.' I have seen men look far more happy and peaceful when dead than ever during their life. In this case I had no idea what he would have been like, for, in the darkness of the stable, I could only distinguish a vague black something at the end of the stall, but could not make out a single detail Before leaving the stable, I glanced at the stall once again, wondering who it could be, for, strange to say, the thought of Ned Bolton did not once occur to me I did not know him much, and when I left he was not thought to be dangerously injured, so I had quite forgotten all about his accident. After locking the stables, I went away down to the Sergeant's for tea. There I learnt first of Bolton's death, and the inquest that was to be held so soon as a doctor could come from Lawrence. But the roads were heavy and the rivers high (we had had very hard rain a few days before) so that it might be another day before he arrived. In the meanwhile the body was to remain in the Camp stable. We had tea, and after, a long and jolly chat. Then, as the Sergeant had to go into the town, we left the house and walked up the hill together.

Having reached the Warden's office, he turned off to the township. I paused for a final look round before going to bed. It was a lovely night—frosty, clear, and still. From a cloudless, purple sky, the full moon shed a flood of brightness, shewing every object as clearly as by day. The Argyle Ranges, furrowed by many a deep gully where blue shadows lay, curved round to meet the Dome Peak, that shone all sparkling with snow above the line of dark birch bush. From the Camp, you know, one can see right on beyond the semi-circular valley at the racecourse and the little hill at the back, across the flat, with the wrinkled hills upon, each leading up to the loftier mountains which in the winter shut in. the view with a snowy wall. I like nice scenery, and it is worth while to stand for half-an-hour, even on a frosty night, to see the Waikaia curving like a silver band through the long grey plain. Turning round, I noticed some waggoners had camped just beyond the fluming, and their horses, some of them with bells on, were feeding close by. 'I hope,' said I to myself, 'that those tarnation brutes won't be coming and tramping round the house with those jangling bells to keep one awake, and to make sure, I drove them down the road before I went to bed.

I locked the front door, turning the inside catch as well, and also fastened my bedroom door. But I could not sleep. The rush of the water down the race disturbed me, the still dead-ness of the frosty night made me wakeful, and I was the more so when I could hear, faintly at first, but gradually coming nearer, the sharp tinkling horsebells. The brutes came on, and were presently champing the fresh grass by the door, rubbing themselves against the walls and stamping about, while with each movement the bells jangled again. At last it got past endurance, and partly dressing myself, I went out and drove them far away down the road. The keen frosty air thoroughly roused me, and I lay in my bed knocking from side to side, or watching the moonlight streaming through the window.

Presently I was startled by what appeared to be the figure of a man going slowly past the window. It struck me the more, because, though I could see it plainly enough, yet I fancied it did not seem to intercept the light, to cast no shadow, to be transparent, in fact. Before I had time to reason about the matter, I heard the front door opening—it creaks, you know—and felt the draught of the keen night air. Then my bedroom door opened, and a figure glided in. I can't say walked in, for the lower limbs were motionless—it seemed to drift along. It came on, and stopped at my bed's-head. I crushed myself against the wall as close as possible, and looked in wonder at this uncanny visitor.

The figure was that of a man about my own height, but of slighter build. The hands lay stiff and close against the sides; the face I could not see. It was concealed by a canvas bag that came low down beneath the shoulders, and there was a string fastened round the neck. I had not been able to distinguish any of these particulars in the dark stable, you remember. I looked at it long and treadily, and shrank still closer to the wall as it began slowly to bend down towards me. It came down closer and closer, till the face was near my own, then I put up my hands to thrust it off. It was no shadowy substance I encountered, but a heavy, dead, stiff form that pressed down on me. I seized it near the shoulders, could distinctly touch the canvass wrapper, could recognize that nameless horror that one feels when touching a corpse, and with all my might fought against it, trying to keep it off. Suddenly it straightened itself, glided from my bedside and was gone.

In vain I tried to persuade myself it was all a dream, and that the big drops of perspiration on my forehead were the effects of mental agony. No, I was awake—thoroughly, wide awake; and though I searched everywhere, and this directly, the figure had gone. I could find no one hidden who might have played me so cruel a trick. I could hear voices in the town, and looking down the hill could see a light in the Sergeant's house.

For a time I had some thought of going there and telling them what I had seen; but, reflecting on the matter, who would believe me? I could only say that the figure of a man dead, stiff, and cold, had come into my room, that I had wrestled with it, and it had vanished. Was it a credible story? No, they would only laugh, and hint, perhaps, that I was not sober. In fact, standing there in the moonlight, with familiar objects close at hand, I began to doubt my own experience. It must have been a dream, I said to myself, and so went to bed again. But not to sleep. I heard the noises more disturbingly than ever. Listening, yet trying not to hear, I caught the faint tinkle of the bells, each moment becoming sharper and more distressing. At last the horses were again close to the door and rubbing against the house. I sat up, meaning to go and turn them away, when again the same ominous shadow slipped past the window, and breathlessly I waited, till, with a breath of frosty air, and through the creaking doors, it passed into my room. Now, there could be no mistake.

I saw it as plainly as I see you and, when it stopped and bent towards me, I grappled with its cold, dead weight, and touched the canvass round its head as plainly as I touch you now. (Don't jump, old boy; I'm not a ghost.) Well, as at first, the struggle was hard and fierce. It pressed close down as if it wished to place its damp, dead face beside mine, then suddenly sprang aside, and was gone. I lay there thoroughly mystified. I knew now I was not asleep. Outside, I could hear the horses jingling their bells, and the water sweeping down the race. There, too, was every object in my room to be plainly seen. I rose, wiped the perspiration from my fore-head, and going out, I chased the horses away, walked about a bit, then, looking at my watch, found it was past one o'clock. The town was silent; the light was gone from the Sergeant's house, so I walked up and down inside my room waiting for the dawn. It was twenty minutes past two when I heard the horses again coming slowly up the hill. They kept coming closer and closer, tramping round and round, rubbing against the house, and always with, the accompaniment of the sharp, discordant bells. At first, the noise and movement were comforting in contrast to the horror of that dead thing, but by and bye the clanking became intolerable, and I was just on the point of going out, when again the shadow glided past the window.

Now, I was thoroughly prepared, and sat up in bed. It came in and stopped beside me. I saw it as clearly as I now see you,—the stiff unbending form with the canvass round the shoulders, which were sharply outlined through the wrapper, and the string round its neck. I don't know why, but these details seemed to strike me most. It bent down towards me, and now such a struggle began as I never had in my life before and do not wish for again. I was determined to find out what the thing was, and had grasped it by the shoulders. I am as strong as most men, but I was powerless against this. It crushed me down on my bed.

I held fast. It moved away, and we struggled through the room till we came to where my box stood in a corner. It forced me down on that, bent me backwards over it, pressing me harder and harder, closer and closer, then suddenly it slipped from my grasp and was gone. I lay a minute or so panting after the terrible struggle; then, having dressed myself, went out.

No more attempts at sleep for me; and I was not sorry when the first golden flash of dawn brightened the sky. As soon as the light was strong I went into the stable, and there, at the upper end of the stall, lay the dead body, with canvass wrapped about the shoulders, which stuck out sharply, a string being tied round the neck, in every particular just as it has appeared to me during the night. That's my ghost story, Harry, and I can neither explain nor understand it. The dead man was no friend of mine, hardly to be called an acquaintance. He was buried late next day, and I saw no more of him either by dark or daylight However, lad, I can tell you this: I always hated those sharp tinkling horse-bells, but more than ever since that night, for now a shudder always comes across me at the sound.'

"'And well it may do, Pater,' I replied. 'Still, is it not possible that, in spite of its seeming reality, it was only a very vivid and hideous nightmare after all?"

"'Tarnation! don't I tell you I was wide awake—had I never once closed my eyes or lost consciousness. No, you can't explain the matter in that way.'

"'And as for drinking, I suppose——'

"'Suppose what you please,' interrupted the Pater, getting angry now. 'I had but one drink all day, just before starting down the Gorge and after a ride of 35 miles through a keen, wintry afternoon could have little effect.'

'Well, it is the queerest thing I ever heard of, I can't understand it — but — er. Er —'

"'Confound your inconsequential 'buts.' If you have any objection to make, make it.'

"'No, oh no; I was merely going to say as before, that it is quite beyond me.'

"'H'm'n. If you live to be as old as I am, lad, you will find there are a good many 'more things in heaven and earth than are dreamt of in your philosophy.'

"Such is the Pater's Ghost Story, boys. He was as brave and true a fellow as ever breathed, and though he could never find any reason for it, you may take my word he did see all this exactly as I have told you."

"Ah!" said Harry Clare, "it's all mighty fine to talk about ghosts, wait till you've got realities in the shape of a dozen youngsters to think of, and you'll have no call to be afraid of ghosts. Are you ready for home, Archie?"

"Will, look here, Harry, I don't half like that ghost story, and besides, it is very wet and dark outside, I think I'll get a bed here to-night."

"Now, I do call that real mean," ejaculated Harry, "to let a fellow walk home alone through the dark, after telling him a blessed yarn fit to frighten _____ "

"Oh, but you don't believe in ghosts or such things," said Archie.

"No, that I don't," was Harry's defiant reply, "and so I'm off, and a very good night, boys, one and all."

The End.

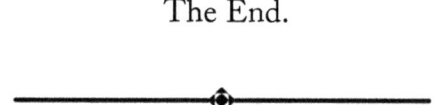

Bibliography

Primary Sources
"We Four, and the Stories We Told." by Henry Lapham – Printed by *"Otago Daily Times"* Dowling Street. 1880.

Newspapers
Otago Witness.
Illustrated London news.

Secondary sources
Waikaia (the Golden Century 1860-1962) F.W.G Miller
The Bibliography of Australian Literature -John Arnold & John Hay 2009

Image Sources
Henry Lapham - *Otago Witness* – Sourced Papers Past – February 6th 1901
The Illustrated London News
Map of Waikaia and part of Wart Hill Survey Districts, 1889 drawn by W..Deverell, October 1889. Courtesy of P. Diver.

Websites
Papers Past – www.paperspast.natlib.govt.nz/
NZ ETC – www.nzetc.victoria.ac.nz/
State Library Of Victoria. www.slv.vic.gov.au
Dictionary of New Zealand Biographywww.teara.govt.nz/en/biographies

Index

Alexandra..4
alluvial gold...4
Australia...3
Campbell's..4
Central Otago...4
Chinese miners..5
Dome Peak..49
Donnybrook...48
Dunedin..44
Dunstan...4
Frenchman's Hill...26
Gow's Creek..27
Harry Clare..54
Henry Lapham..3
Invercargill..3
King Solomon's Mine.......................................5
Lawrence...49

Michael Brennan......................................25, 44
Milestone..21, 22
Ned Bolton...48
Nevis..48
Nokomai..25, 38, 48
Otago...3
Otago Witness,..3
Potter's..4
Switzers...4, 5, 25, 26, 27, 44
The Argyle Ranges..49
The Crown Hotel......................................26, 27, 38, 44
The Hill...38
Tuapeka...4
United States Hotel......................................14
Waikaia...3, 4, 25, 26, 49
Winding Creek..26

www.ingramcontent.com/pod-product-compliance
Lightning Source LLC
Chambersburg PA
CBHW070108100426
42743CB00012B/2684